SEARCH-AND-RESCUE
ANIMALS

Lisa Idzikowski

Enslow Publishing

E

101 W. 23rd Street
Suite 240
New York, NY 10011
USA

enslow.com

WORDS TO KNOW

cadaver dogs Dogs that search for people who have died.

canine A dog or having to do with dogs.

docile Tame.

equine Having to do with horses.

handler Person who works with a search-and-rescue animal.

K-9 Dogs that work for the military or police force.

monastery A place for prayer, where monks, nuns, and other religious people live.

scent A smell.

volunteer Person who does work for no money.

CONTENTS

Introduction

A Saint Bernard dog named Barry lived more than two hundred years ago. His home was a monastery high up in the mountains between Switzerland and Italy. Snowy Saint Bernard's Pass was nearby. It was a well-liked spot for hikers. In the winter, workers from the monastery guided people through the pass. Soon, the monastery's watchdogs joined in. That's when the monks of St. Bernard's discovered their dogs were so smart. They could find the way through storms. They could walk through deep snow. And that's not all. The dogs even found people buried under thick snow!

How could the dogs do that? The monks guessed that their Saint Bernards had very good noses. People have a scent all their own. Their dogs could smell it. Soon, teams of two or three dogs were searching up and down the snowy trails if someone went missing. When

This Saint Bernard dog looks right at home in the snowy mountains of Italy.

Fact
In 1880, the name "Saint Bernard" was given to these dogs by the Swiss Kennel Club

they smelled someone under the snow, the dogs started digging. They dug and dug until the person was freed.

In 1897, one of the dogs pulled an almost-frozen twelve-year-old boy to safety. Through the years, the dogs of Saint Bernard's were busy. They saved about two thousand people. And according to local stories, Barry saved forty-one of them himself!

What about search and rescue today? The modern-day search-and-rescue system in the United States began around 1960. It started with a group of people who owned German shepherd dogs. These dogs learned to follow trails of human scent. They followed scent in the air

Name That Dog!

At one time, dogs like Barry were called mountain dogs, hospice dogs, Swiss Alpine dogs, and even Barry dogs.

German shepherd dogs were some of the first animals used in search-and-rescue work.

and found lost people. Members of this canine training group formed the American Rescue Dog Association. Some years later, other groups got together. These groups now include both dogs and horses. Have fun learning about these dogs and other animals who help in search and rescue!

Search-and-Rescue Dogs

Terrible things sometimes happen. Skiers might be buried in mounds of snow. Boaters can tip over in fast water. Hikers may become lost in the wilderness. Victims can be trapped under falling buildings. At times like these, search-and-rescue dog teams jump into action!

Breed All About It

Dogs from certain breeds are generally chosen for SAR teams. German shepherds, golden retrievers, Labrador retrievers, Newfoundlands, Belgian Malinois, and bloodhounds are commonly trained to become search-and-rescue dogs.

Brittany spaniels are smart dogs trained for sporting, hunting, and tracking.

A search-and-rescue, or SAR, team is made up of two members. There is a person, or handler, and their specially trained dog. Can any kind of dog be part of a team? Certain types of dogs commonly become search-and-rescue dogs. Think of working dogs usually used for hunting and herding. They are smart. They are

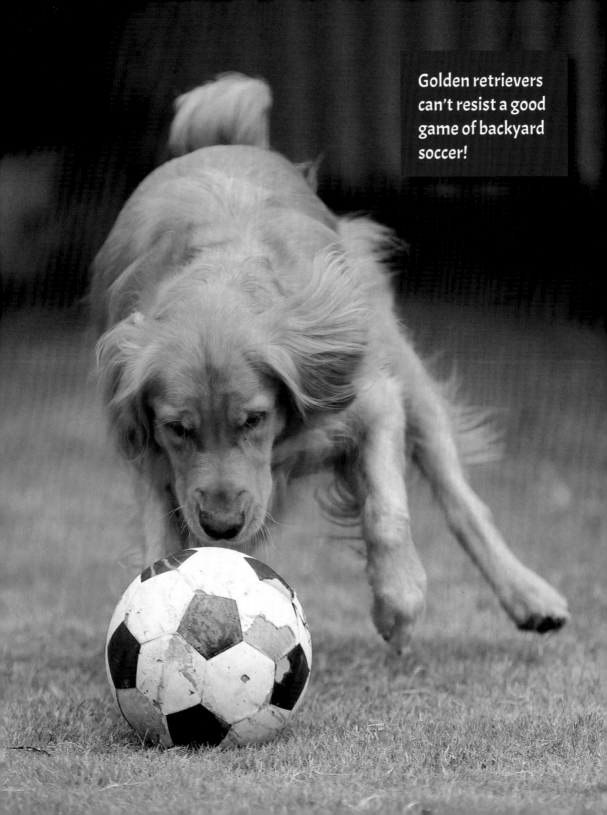

Golden retrievers can't resist a good game of backyard soccer!

friendly. They are strong on their feet. These dogs can be trained to help find people and things.

Dogs trained for search-and-rescue work are alike in certain ways. They have lots of energy. Their senses of sight and hearing are very sharp. And what a nose! With a strong sense of smell, search-and-rescue dogs can notice different odors. These animals also enjoy playing. All these talents help to get the dogs in top shape for their important work.

Fact
It can take almost two years for a dog to be trained to work in search and rescue.

When it's time to work, SAR dogs mind their handlers. They follow orders and understand directions. Handlers speak to their dogs. They also may use hand signals to guide their talented dogs. Do these animals really understand what is being said to them? Dog owners say yes! And science is backing up their claims.

Scientists are looking for answers to this question. By studying the brains of dogs, they are getting ideas. Dogs understand people by hearing both the words and the way those words are spoken, like softly or loudly.

Labrador retrievers are excellent working dogs. They can be trained to do many types of jobs.

Search-and-rescue dogs work hard. They jump, run, dig, swim, and scout—sometimes in the worst possible places. And with their handlers, they help find missing people!

Other Animals
Saving Lives

Move over dogs, and make room for horses and rats! When search-and-rescue teams are needed, horses can gallop into action. Equine, or horse, teams are like search-and-rescue dog teams. Both include a handler and an animal. And these teams also help find missing people.

Long ago, most horses were wild. They lived out in nature, and their senses kept them alive. As wild animals, horses listened and watched for signs of danger. They ran from enemies. They sniffed out places to find food and

The Air-Scenting Horse

El Ninos Poco was the first official air-scenting horse in the United States. He was trained in search-and-rescue work.

water. Later on, people trained horses. Native Americans hunted with horses. Farmers used horses for hard work around farms. People got from place to place on horses.

But what about using horses for search and rescue? Some trainers say horses are the best-kept secret in the world. Horses make great search-and-rescue animals. They can search large amounts of land in a short time.

People work with horses and learn to trust the animals' sense of smell.

Rats are mammals with a sharp sense of smell.

They get in and around where cars cannot go. They carry people, equipment, and supplies. Horses even have as good a sense of smell as dogs.

Fact
African giant pouched rats are calm, docile, and easy to tame.

Handlers learn to understand signs from their horses. Suddenly their animal's ears move. Does the horse hear something? Signs from the horse may guide the team to a missing person.

Picture this. A small, brown, furry animal comes to the rescue. It creeps and crawls into small spaces. It may carry machinery on its back. It likes bananas. It's a rescue…rat?

For more than ten years, rats have been trained to sniff out land mines and disease. Trainers are wondering if these rats can be used in other ways. Could they find buried people? Maybe. African giant rats have good noses like dogs. They climb, run, and root around in small spaces. Why couldn't these rats poke through broken-down buildings? More training is needed. But rats may soon be finding search-and-rescue work.

Search-and-Rescue School for Dogs, Horses, and Rats

Search-and-rescue teams save people's lives. They may make it look easy. But it's not! Handlers and their animals practice for hours and hours. They train when it's warm, cold, sunny, and snowy. Some handlers are emergency workers, such as firefighters and police officers. Most are private citizens. They volunteer their efforts because they want to help others.

Come, sit, and stay. Young puppies often learn these words. Many owners teach their pets these

Handler 101

People who work with SAR animals also get training. They learn skills to help find their way in the wilderness. And they learn how to give first aid to injured people.

A dog in training has a special connection to its handler.

basic manners. They want dogs that are friendly, nice, and not always barking. But what about future search-and-rescue dogs? "Find him," "show me," and "leave it"—these are a few commands

Certain playful puppies will be chosen to be trained as search-and-rescue dogs.

common to search-and-rescue work. With practice, a search-and-rescue dog will learn to understand and obey these words.

Some pups begin training at eight to twelve weeks old. In one kind of training, pups play hide-and-seek. They have lots of fun finding toys. Little by little, pups get better at the game. Find the toy soon turns into find the person. All the while, pups are learning to trust their noses. With practice, they learn how their strong sense of smell can locate people. Older dogs can also go to search-and-rescue school. Sometimes they take longer to learn the skills needed. But once they catch on, they make great team members.

Horses and rats also have a great sense of smell. With practice they can learn to search for certain odors. Horse trainers work with both horses and riders. They teach horses to find and follow human scent in the air. And they teach riders to know their horses to

Fact
Horses depend on their sense of smell as much as humans do on language, according to some experts

Riders can cover large areas and long distances on horseback.

understand when their animal has found something.

Imagine training rats! People in Africa and the United States are having success. African giant rats are learning to find just the right smell. When they do, they get a prize. They work for peanuts and bananas.

So Much Work to Do

More than eighty years ago, in 1937, Amelia Earhart tried to achieve a record. She planned to fly her plane around the world. It would be the first time for a woman! Sadly, she never made it. What happened? People have been trying to figure that out ever since. In June of 2017, a group of dogs and their handlers set sail. They headed for a tiny island in the Pacific Ocean. These specially trained search-and-rescue cadaver dogs were heading for a job. They would search the island for signs of long-lost Amelia Earhart.

Cadaver searches are just one of the special jobs for search-and-rescue dogs. They search for dead bodies. Whatever the job, a dogs' perfect sense of smell makes it all possible. Sometimes children suddenly go missing.

Law enforcement officers often work with trailing and tracking dogs.

The Lifeguard Dog

Newfoundland dogs make great water-rescue K-9s. Known for years as the "lifeguard" dog, they are big, friendly, and strong. Webbed feet and thick fur make them natural swimmers.

Trailing and tracking dogs could be called to help. They are trained to sniff for and follow a certain scent. How does the dog know? The dog sniffs an item belonging to the child, like a toy or hat. Aha! The dog then knows what scent it is searching for.

Many times, search-and-rescue dogs are not searching for a certain person. Instead they are sniffing the air for any human scent. Suppose a hunter gets lost in the forest. A wilderness search-and-rescue K-9 will run through the woods. The dog finds and follows the scent to its origin. Hopefully, the lost hunter is found.

At times disasters occur. Hurricanes and tornadoes are natural disasters. Sometimes buildings fall. What if a home is destroyed? People might be trapped inside.

A dog's powerful nose can locate scents, even in the snow.

Maybe they are underneath and can't get out. Disaster dogs come and search for hurt or trapped people. These dogs also work at disaster sites where the problems are caused by criminals or terrorists.

Fact
Experienced dogs can find people buried under 13 feet (4 meters) of snow.

In the winter, skiers can't wait to head out to their favorite spots. Most days, everyone has fun and stays safe. But what if an avalanche occurs? Some search-and-rescue dogs are trained to work in deep snow. They sniff out people in the snow and come to their rescue!

Search and Rescue in the Future

Think about the damage that earthquakes cause. Buildings fall. Roads cave in. Homes are destroyed. When the call goes out, search-and-rescue teams rush to help. Dogs sniff around and horses walk through debris. Handlers get ready to give first aid.

What if a search-and-rescue animal could creep down under the mess? Way, deep down in the dark. Imagine an animal that could slip and slide into tiny cracks and never get hurt themselves. There may be a

A Snake's Slither

Scientists and engineers have found that sidewinder rattlesnakes can slide and slither even going uphill. Studying the movements of animals helps in designing robots.

problem, though. Some people might find this perfect-sounding search-and-rescue helper too creepy!

Some scientists are building robot-roaches for the future of search and rescue. They fit live cockroaches with special backpacks. Scientists can then control the insects' movements. As the robot-roaches creep and crawl, they listen for sounds. Scientists think these special insects could someday do a special job. They could find people trapped under buildings who are calling for help!

To solve problems, engineers might study animals in nature, like snakes!

Engineers have some ideas about search-and-rescue work, too. They are working on making another kind of robot. What could really help with search and rescue, they wondered? They studied different kinds of animals and decided on snakes. They made a robot that can climb, swim, and crawl like a snake. Disaster sites are full of danger. In the future, robots may be able to work in places where it is unsafe to send in dog or horse search-and-rescue teams.

Fact
Cockroaches are so tough they can live for days even if their heads are cut off!

Learn More

Books

Bozzo, Linda. *Search And Rescue Dog Heroes.* Berkeley Heights, NJ: Enslow Publishers, Inc., 2011.

McKenzie, Precious. *Search and Rescue Animals.* North Mankato, MN: Rourke Educational Media, 2015.

Zeiger, Jennifer. *Animals Helping After Disaster.* New York, NY: Scholastic Inc., 2015.

Websites

American Kennel Club
http://www.akc.org/dog-owners/training/canine-good-citizen
Learn about basic manners for dogs at the AKC's site for Canine Good Citizen.

Discovery Kids
http://discoverykids.com/category/pets
Learn all about search-and-rescue dogs.

INDEX

Published in 2019 by Enslow Publishing, LLC.
101 W. 23rd Street, Suite 240, New York, NY 10011

Copyright © 2019 by Enslow Publishing, LLC.

Library of Congress Cataloging-in-Publication Data

Names: Idzikowski, Lisa, author.
Title: Search-and-rescue animals / Lisa Idzikowski.
Description: New York : Enslow Publishing, [2019] | Series: Animals at work | Audience: Grade 3-6. | Includes bibliographical references and index.
Identifiers: LCCN 2017051999| ISBN 9780766096233 (library bound) | ISBN 9780766096240 (paperback) | ISBN 9780766096257 (6 pack)
Subjects: LCSH: Working animals—Juvenile literature. | Search dogs—Juvenile literature. | Rescue dogs—Juvenile literature.
Classification: LCC SF172 .I39 2019 | DDC 636.73—dc23
LC record available at https://lccn.loc.gov/2017051999

Printed in the United States of America

To Our Readers: We have done our best to make sure all website addresses in this book were active and appropriate when we went to press. However, the author and the publisher have no control over and assume no liability for the material available on those websites or on any websites they may link to. Any comments or suggestions can be sent by e-mail to customerservice@enslow.com.

Photo Credits: Cover, p. 1 Thinkstock/Stockbyte/Getty Images; p. 5 © StefaMi/iStock/Thinkstock; p. 7 Peter Kunasz/Shutterstock.com; p. 9 CyberKat/Shutterstock.com; p. 10 Wasitt Hemwarapornchai/Shutterstock.com; p. 12 SG Shot/Shutterstock.com; p. 14 © Mlenny/Thinkstock; p. 15 Vicuschka/Shutterstock.com; p. 16 Africa Studio/Shutterstock.com; p. 19 Pavel L Photo and Video/Shutterstock.com; p. 20 Sundays Photography/Shutterstock.com; p. 22 © TerryJ/Thinkstock; p. 24 Arterra Picture Library/Alamy Stock Photo; p. 26 Melica/Shutterstock.com; p. 29 science photo/Shutterstock.com; p. 30 Volodymyr Pylypchuk/Shutterstock.com.